BREAKING NEW GROUND
CHURCH PLANTING IN THE CHURCH OF ENGLAND

A report commissioned by the House of Bishops
of the General Synod of the Church of England

GS 1099

CHURCH HOUSE PUBLISHING
Church House, Great Smith Street, London SW1P 3NZ

ISBN 0 7151 3759 X

Published 1994 for the General Synod of the Church of England by Church House Publishing

Printed in England by Orphans Press.

BOARD OF MISSION

WORKING PARTY ON CHURCH PLANTING

At the request of the Standing Committee of the House of Bishops a workshop on church planting was held during the June 1991 Bishops' Meeting. Twenty-one Bishops attended and identified areas where further work needed to be done.

At the October 1991 meeting of the House of Bishops' Standing Committee the Board of Mission was asked to set up a Working Party on Church Planting which would report to the House.

Membership of the Working Party has been as follows:

The Rt Rev. Patrick Harris, (Chairman)	The Bishop of Southwell
The Rev. Ian Bunting	Director of Ordinands, Diocese of Southwell
Mrs Terry Garley	Ecumenical Officer for Derbyshire and Nottinghamshire
The Rev. George Lings	Vicar, St George's Deal
The Rt Rev. Christopher Mayfield,	The Bishop of Manchester
The Rt Rev. Peter Selby	William Leech Professorial Fellow in Applied Theology, University of Durham
Miss Cynthia Sutherland	Member of General Synod Committee for Black Anglican Concerns
The Rev. Canon Philip King (Secretary)	General Secretary, General Synod Board of Mission
Dr Anne Richards	Mission Theology Secretary, General Synod Board of Mission

AN INTRODUCTORY LETTER FROM THE CHAIRMAN

Planting new congregations enables churches to reach out with a locally accessible centre of Christian worship, witness and service.

New Church of England and ecumenical congregations are springing up all over the country, in fact the average rate since 1990 has been one church plant per fortnight. Sometimes they are a part of a parish's mission strategy and operate within the boundaries of that parish. At other times, with diocesan approval, they reach out beyond their boundaries to underchurched neighbourhoods, and even to networks of people with cultural or ethnic links in common. In nearly every case, church planting has attracted interest and support, and has caused few problems. In a few cases, no more than four that we are aware of, new congregations have been planted without the approval of the bishop and the local clergy. It was these cases, and the questions they raised, which led the House of Bishops to appoint the Working Party.

The conclusion of the present report is that the structures and Canons of the Church of England are flexible enough to allow bishops to encourage and to enable church planting to take place in their dioceses. Where there is goodwill on all sides, new congregations can be planted even across the boundaries of parishes, deaneries and dioceses. This report also highlights the potential of deaneries to become very significant units in terms of mission strategy and sharing of resources.

However, this report does not avoid the difficult cases which cause anxiety to both Bishops and local clergy. The best way to tackle problems, we believe, is to face up to, and address the issues, before confrontation arises. It is important here, and indeed in all cases, that personal contact and consultation should be made alongside correspondence. The stories of church planting in the report demonstrate many of the principles which are at stake, such as the legal position of church plants, the authorization of leaders, the use of buildings, relationships within the diocese and with other Churches, permitted forms of worship and Anglican identity. The report offers guidance both to those who want to encourage church planting and to those who face the hard questions which arise inevitably when the Church breaks new ground to plant congregations.

One lesson to be learned is strikingly clear. Church planting calls for collaborative ministry. There is no room either for aggressive empire building or for last ditch defensiveness. A collaborative approach based on respect and mutual interdependence helps to eliminate the sense of threat which can accompany a new initiative. Above all, it encourages sensitivity to others and an awareness that the mission of the Church is all of a piece. The Working Party believes that in this Decade of Evangelism, church planting makes a significant contribution by providing a mission-oriented opportunity to practise collaborative ministry.

Finally, the working party believes that church planting is not an erosion of the parish principle of mission in the Church of England. It is a *supplementary* strategy which enhances the essential thrust of the parish principle - a commitment to a ministry to all members of the community, individually and collectively, within the overall commitment to establishing and sustaining the Kingdom of God.

+ Patrick Southwell

CONTENTS

Part One

CHURCH PLANT: OPPORTUNITY OR DANGER?

A Vision of Church: Territory, Neighbourhood and Network

1.1 When a congregation looks outward in mission, and considers strategies for evangelism, it may be that some of the most exciting possibilities for that parish involve planting a new church. Indeed, we already know of 177 church plants which have come about since statistics began to be collected in 1985. However, such a strategy is not itself particularly new in the Church of England, and has a given history; therefore church planting will, we hope, be adopted as an appropriate method of evangelism in many situations.

1.2 Those instances where such a strategy has involved crossing the established boundary of a parish or diocese have now thrown a spotlight on to the whole concept and practice of church planting. Such cross-boundary plants are still few in number and are likely always to remain a minority; however these examples raise important questions about the role of territory in the self-understanding of the Church of England. In response to the concern generated in the recipient parishes and dioceses, these important questions stand to be addressed.

1.3 Part of the concern is due to the long association between ministry and jurisdiction over territory. It is not just a case of a desire to maintain traditional patterns of power and authority, but rather that territory also has had a significant effect in guaranteeing the theological diversity of the Church of England: diversity feels safer if we know it will be contained within certain areas and will not 'stray'. Where territorial boundaries are respected there can be a greater willingness, paradoxically, to allow patterns of worship and presentations of belief that would otherwise not be accepted if it were thought that these could happen anywhere. The same is true when a local ecumenical project is established. The notion that the maintenance of boundaries permits freedoms within limits is now encountering resistance from those whose concern it is to forward an acceptance of the rich variety of ways in which

1

Christian belief is expressed in the Church of England, in Churches Together, and in other congregations in this country.

1.4 This rich variety further points to the heterogeneity of the Church, which although often unstated, is now understood to be a fundamental part of its witness. There exists an assumption that congregations will in most cases be made up of people of a variety of ages, classes, ethnicity and gender. Another facet of the concern, therefore, is a perception that church plants are homogeneous at their inception and therefore not of a piece with the heterogeneity of the Body of Christ. This does not take into account, however, the process of maturation which plants undergo. Many congregations which are initially homogeneous grow into the acceptance of variety and difference which we expect within the Church of England as a whole. Further, it is necessary to point out that not all Anglican congregations are particularly heterogeneous and only some church plants are distinctively homogeneous.

1.5 Because of the traditional link between parish and territory, church planting across parish or diocesan boundaries has caused concern in very similar ways to that engendered by inter-parochial agencies such as training or social responsibility departments, or by industrial mission, working within dioceses. In these cases, it is easy for the parishes and clergy of the neighbourhood to feel caught up in a process which will involve having certain theological outlooks imposed on them.[1]

1.6 Nevertheless, at certain points – and such points have been crucial for the development of the life of the Church – the 'territorial contract' breaks down under the pressure of new thinking or convictions which in the nature of things, cannot accept territorial limitation. Such new thinking has arisen as a result of population movements, especially in urban settings, causing traditional parish boundaries in some places to become irrelevant anachronisms. This may also be the case where several churches of different denominations have joined together to establish a common witness in a particular place. Typically, we may see that church

---

[1] Here, we may note that the experience of planting across denominational rather than territorial boundaries has led to the publication of guidelines: *Constitutional Guidelines for a Local Ecumenical Project,* issued by the Consultative Committee for LEPs in England, January 1990. This document refers to the creation of 'new relationships in the context of existing ones' (p.3), a concept which is important for successful church planting.

planting across parish and diocesan boundaries has happened under the pressure of an evangelistic imperative that has assumed precedence over loyalty to the institution and its territorial contract.

1.7   When we face the pressure of such moments – the urgency of the *kairos* – we have to respond. The reality that active members of the Church of England might prefer ecclesiastical traditions different from those dominant in their territorially defined parish church is recognized in the gift of full parochial rights to members of church electoral rolls. There is at present a movement to recognize other developments in communities which similarly cross parish boundaries. Therefore it is possible to see that it is networks which are now the communities to which we feel a predominant loyalty. Churches for the deaf, student congregations and African, Afro-Caribbean and Asian congregations would be examples. We may say, then, that many in the Church of England, and not just those involved in church planting, are asking for recognition that human life is lived in a complex array of networks and that the neighbourhoods where people reside may hold only a very minor loyalty.

1.8   In his address to the Church Planting Conference in 1991, the Archbishop of Canterbury said: 'Our Anglican understanding of the church is rooted in episcopal leadership and parochial structure'.[2] The church planting movement makes an important contribution to the ongoing debate about how these features of the life of the Church of England are lived out in contemporary society, and how that life can be accessible to the widest range of people. The episcopate represents the Church's catholicity, while the parochial structure has been the means of ensuring that the Church is earthed in the life of the community and accepts responsibility for all. This means attending to the fact that such rootedness in the community may need to express itself in ways that go beyond the bounds of the territorial parish. It also means taking seriously the ways in which community exists in networks of relationship and not just in territorial closeness.

1.9   We need therefore to find ways to enable diverse styles of church life to co-exist without always having recourse to territorial, or even

---

[2] George Carey and others, *Planting New Churches – Guidelines and Structures for Developing Tomorrow's Churches*, ed. Bob Hopkins, Eagle, Guildford 1991, p.25.

denominational, boundaries, and here the church planting movement has much to teach us. Further, an episcopal church is well placed to discern when, in order to be rooted in the community, the focus on parochial territory needs supplementing with a realistic awareness of network and neighbourhood. Where a church plant is proposed, the bishop or bishops concerned may be in a position to look at the mission of the Church of England over a wider area, as well as to appreciate the reasons for the sense of threat which a recipient parish may feel. Contemporary mission is now demanding this kind of recognition and discussion, as well as openness to more collaboration between parishes and between people. In such situations, the assertion that parish boundaries are paramount will merely paralyse initiative.

1.10 An understanding of evangelisation that embraces the whole of our individual and corporate life has to move in a direction that takes seriously the neighbourhoods and networks in which we live. This understanding must include partner churches in a corporate vision of Christian unity: the whole people of God. In this sense, we may regard church plants as illustrating the outworking of the theological principles of Christian mission but not contrary to an understanding of mission which sees the Church of England as a church for all the people, both individually and corporately. On the other hand, this understanding of evangelisation must also take seriously the need for coherence, for the gospel is not simply a licence to pursue individual enthusiasms. It should not lead to sectarianism, triumphalism, endorsement of a consumer approach to mission, or threaten the historic order and institution of the Church. It is for this reason that we are asking those keen to plant churches to place their ideas before their bishop for wider consideration at an early stage and to ask their bishop for responsive leadership and guidance. Bishops do have real opportunities here to support and encourage mission in their dioceses. We are also asking bishops to establish consultative bodies in their dioceses. This is first to facilitate initiatives by dioceses but also to allow sensitivity to other Church of England and partner churches in the area. It will also ensure that mechanisms are in place to deal with practical implications without crushing the vitality or zeal that brought them into being.

Part Two

WHAT ARE CHURCH PLANTS LIKE?

2.1 Definitions

In referring to 'planting churches' or to a 'church plant' in this report, the word 'church' indicates a part of the Christian community, the Body of Christ, as opposed to the connotations of the word as building or structure, *even though* buildings or structures may be involved. In this sense, the word 'church' has specifically a 'network' rather than 'territory' association, and has been defined for the purposes of this report as: 'a group of Christians predominantly drawn from a discernible neighbourhood, culture or network who are led by those with authorization from the wider Church, whose worship and common life includes regular commitment to preaching the Word and to the celebration of the two dominical sacraments'.

2.2   The word 'plant', however, has more associations with territory, since it implies a locus where the new congregation is situated. However, in the phrase 'church planting' there is a conflation of meanings, in that the phrase simultaneously implies a section of the worshipping community of people and a located place and/or building. The 'planting' part of the phrase refers specifically to the transposition of the first into the second. This is a very special characteristic of this activity and argues strongly for maintaining the phrase at all times as two words.

2.3   In order to describe the phenomenon of church planting it may be helpful to produce some defining characteristics. It is important however, to recognize that there can be no definitive set of criteria, since church planting is an organic, living process.[3] For this reason, this report offers not only the following characteristics of church plants, but also a set of analogies for the different kinds of church plant which may be encountered, and these are set out below.

---

[3] This living process is reflected in the familial imagery which is of typical usage and also employed in this document, for example: 'parent', 'daughter', 'sister' church.

2.4 Some usual characteristics of a church plant:

(a) it arises from a conscious evangelistic purpose to inaugurate a congregation;

(b) it involves the transfer of people from an initial congregation to create or to revitalize another congregation; transfer of people may also occur from several congregations, especially in the case of an ecumenical plant;

(c) it has a known corporate identity and style;

(d) it has an identified leadership, which is recognized by others inside and outside the plant;

(e) it has identifiable pastoral structures;

(f) it is intended to serve an identifiable group, culture or neighbourhood.

2.5 Types of church plant

A number of factors determine the various types of church plant. These include: the size of the planting team, what partnerships are involved, whether team members relocate and what gap has to be bridged in order to produce effective outreach. These types of church plant are categorized according to horticultural images in order to point up the fact that church planting is an intrinsically living process.[4]

2.5.i RUNNER

A 'Runner' represents a church plant in which there is the closest link possible between the parent body and the new entity. Its meeting place falls within the originating parish and the planting team is made up exclusively of members from the parent church. No other parish is directly involved. All plants falling within the originating parish may be classed as runners, but may fall into one of two distinct types (see 2.5.vi and vii). We know of around 170 examples.[5]

2.5.ii GRAFT

A 'Graft' refers to a church plant where a planting team has come in from outside the parish, in junior or equal partnership (in terms of size and role)

---

[4] A table for the identification of plants is given in Appendix Two.

[5] A complete set of statistics is given in Appendix Three.

with the receiving parish, to create a fresh overall congregation with a mission emphasis. These are much less common: we know of 27 examples.

2.5.iii TRANSPLANT

A 'Transplant' indicates a church plant in which a coherent team large enough to form an instant congregation is, with permission, transferred across a boundary to a new location. The incoming group will be in senior partnership with any residual receiving congregation. We know of 17 such examples. There are also 4 examples of transplant where the characteristic crossing of a boundary has been unauthorized.

2.5.iv SEED

'Seeds' are those examples of church planting which involve the crossing of geographical and cultural barriers by a small team who physically relocate and form minority partnerships. Separation from the parent body and relocation as an autonomous body at a greater distance is therefore to be expected in this category, and will include preparation akin to that for cross cultural mission partners. This is the least common form of church planting category among Church of England members in Britain.

2.5.v 'Runner', 'Graft' and 'Seed' plants may also be usefully subdivided into two equally distinct types. These reflect different mission challenges as well as the different levels of available resources.

2.5.vi PIONEER

The adjective 'pioneer' indicates that a plant is breaking new ground in moving into an area where no other Church of England congregation is present, or into a network which has had no Anglican presence hitherto. It usually implies a team size in single figures and the members of the team do not relocate. In this respect, the term also points to a particular moment in a congregation's history, being indicative of a plant's genesis or inception.

2.5. vii PROGRESSION

A 'progression' plant differs from a 'pioneer' plant in that it is not involved in forming new relationships within an underchurched area (see Part Three), but is building on relationships which are already established. For example, where members of a housing estate in the corner of a parish already have worshippers at the parish church, those worshippers may come to see the need for a local plant on that estate and thus a plant will arise. The term 'progression' also here indicates that the plant has a slightly more advanced evolutionary status in that it may be more developed in terms of its relationships and processes.

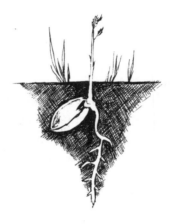

Part Three

WHERE DO CHURCH PLANTS HAPPEN?

3.1   Underchurched areas

The types of church plant (2.5) describe some of the varied responses that may be made in mission, depending on the resources available and on the authorization given. It is equally important also that the areas in greatest need of church plants are clearly identified. One way of doing this is to create designated 'underchurched areas'. Where such areas are identified, a church plant may be the most appropriate strategic response to the particular needs of the communities within such an area.

3.2   There is increasing recognition that in many areas of urban England there are pockets of 2,000-5,000 people who are unchurched for all practical purposes. Undoubtedly, there are also communities of unchurched people in rural areas. The territorial inclusion of such people in the parochial system cannot automatically include them in 'church'. It is noticeable further that 'inadequate penetration of the parish' has been the most common motive for planting during the last fifteen years. Some parishes are aware that underchurched areas exist within their boundaries but do not have the resources to respond. It has therefore been suggested that such identified areas become what the Diocese of Wakefield has called 'Mission Priority Areas' and are given official recognition by dioceses as 'underchurched areas' for which church planting may be an option as part of an overall mission strategy.

3.3   Such official recognition of an area where church planting might form part of a predetermined parish, deanery or indeed diocesan mission strategy would have to take account of at least six factors:

(a)   geographical isolation, caused by roads or railway lines, or cultural isolation, brought about by an incoming population;

(b)   the relationship between church attendance and size of population;

(c)   the home location of church attenders and defined areas without churchgoers;

(d) the presence of a dormant church community caused by diminution of a congregation;

(e) deanery awareness of areas which straddle parish boundaries;

(f) awareness of the strength and vitality of other denominations, churches or Christian groups in the area.

3.4 The process of identifying underchurched areas will require consultation between diocese, deanery, parish and ecumenical partners, with perhaps an outside consultant. When such areas have been identified, this will involve dioceses and others, such as the appropriate Churches Together councils, in giving support and resources to these areas. Church planting will then provide one possibility alongside other strategies involving the disposition of ordained ministers such that underchurched areas have a priority. The creation of Group or Team Ministries between parishes, where one or more or these parishes contains an underchurched area, can be a means of securing the necessary trust and flexibility over boundaries. This may also help to match needs to the resources of a parish or parishes that are in a position to implement such a strategy. With sensitivity and diocesan-led planning it may be possible to enlist the assistance of the neighbouring parish in the Team or Group, where that parish is in a better position to respond. This would be a determining factor for any kind of church plant which might usefully serve that area. This identification of underchurched areas might be done by consultative bodies established in dioceses (see 1.10).

Part Four

HOW DO CHURCH PLANTS WORK?

4.1   In order to understand the potential for church planting, there are a number of factors which need consideration. The statistics regarding church attendance, the current demand on resources available, the economic condition of churches and the numbers of people entering the ministry, all mean that dioceses must now reassess the challenge of the Church's mission.

4.2   These are some of the factors which have forced church planting strategy on to the agenda. Church planting challenges the traditional uses of such resources: new congregations may be planted in unconsecrated buildings such as schools, community centres, public halls and clubs, and they may be led by a member of the clergy or be entirely lay led. Consequently, church plants may be exciting in the way that they are seen to respond to the contemporary climate, but may also be controversial, for example where they expose the need to supplement discrete territorial boundaries to include neighbourhood or network.

4.3   A way of exploring the issues raised by ecclesiological factors and the strategies arising from them, is to review the relationship between the sponsoring and planted congregation. The following examples are illustrative of processes associated with church planting.

4.3.i   THE DUPLICATE SERVICE

The argument for this practice runs as follows: if a church is currently full, then it must be offering an acceptable style of worship. Therefore the service is repeated on a Sunday morning and deliberately remains the same in order to avoid the suggestion of first and second class services. A survey in Administry[6] has shown however, that in seven out of ten cases this strategy

---

[6]   *Administry* (69 Sandridge Road, St Albans, Herts, AL1 4AG) is a consultation service to member churches which exists for 'rediscovering gifts of administration in churches' and which is designed to help churches of all denominations organise and co-ordinate their activities, so as to allow a more effective ministry. The survey was published in Resource Paper 91:3 (August 1991) 'Get up and grow!'.

has been short-lived and has been abandoned, even where it has meant a return to overcrowding. It is observable that this has been an unsuccessful response to the churches' needs and is in fact an administrative adjustment rather than an attempt at a plant proper (see 2.4).

4.3.ii SATELLITE SERVICES

Satellite services have also been described as 'overflow' or 'dispersed' congregations. Where a church is full to capacity and is simultaneously aware that parts of the parish require a local centre of worship, then church planting becomes an option. The strategy usually involves using a public building such as a school or a community centre as a convenient venue and the inhabitants of the neighbourhood are invited to attend. The parish church, or parent church may seek to retain control in the interests of maintaining the unity of the church family. This has tended to create conditions of dependency in the planted church. Although this strategy has sometimes led to an early growth in numbers, such growth has often levelled out and even declined. Consequently, this strategy seems to be most effective where it is seen as a deliberate staging post in a larger vision which includes independent identity for the plant at a later period.

4.3.iii DAUGHTER CHURCH

The Church of England has a history of planting daughter churches which have had a greater degree of autonomy than satellite services. Usually staffed by an ordained priest in a second curacy, they have been given some form of district church council. They have also often benefited from having a clergy house and a building for worship provided at diocesan expense. In practice, daughter churches have often exhibited characteristics of continued immaturity, such that typically, twenty years or more must pass before the daughter church may exhibit a sustained growth to parish status. It would seem possible, that if expectations of the progression to parish status could be more clearly defined and the time-frame for this step shortened, then this could encourage the daughter church to mature more quickly.

4.3.iv MULTIPLE CONGREGATIONS

This strategy should not be confused with that of duplicating services. Usually, the intention is to provide within one church a range of differing styles of worship at the various services. A parish which pursues this path will be made up of separate congregations. The individual identity of each congregation will be welcomed and fully respected. These separate identities may be determined by purpose – for example, to provide an evangelistic 'church for the unchurched'. Or the determining factor may be culture – for example, to provide an informal 'church for the post-60s generation'. Each congregation could have its own leadership and pastoral arrangements although financial management and administration will usually remain centralized. With the current financial constraints, the use of one existing building for multiple congregations may greatly reduce costs. Further, this strategy may offer an attractive route for a parish to plant new churches when there are no clear new geographical neighbourhoods externally available .

4.3.v SHARED BUILDINGS

Many churches already have experience of sharing their buildings – for example, with African, Afro-Caribbean or Asian congregations. However, a logical extension of the multiple congregation strategy may lead to a point where a growing congregation with a distinctive style, or one which appeals to a particular cultural grouping, establishes an independent existence, with its own minister and its own administrative and pastoral structures (see 5.4) This strategy may form an option for some cross boundary plants.[7]

4.3.vi EQUAL PARTNERS

In this strategy, the planted congregation has its own, not necessarily ecclesiastical, building. The church has its own leadership and governmental processes. Although in some cases such plants may not be parishes in their own right or be included in group ministries, their adult identity is ensured by the freedoms conferred upon them by the parent church. In those cases where the new congregation is able to rescue the life of a redundant church, or reverse the fortunes of a congregation in terminal decline, the process of establishing institutional independence can be speeded up.

---

[7] *The Sharing of Church Buildings Act* (1969) still governs ecumenical situations.

4.4   An examination of these strategies shows that the most healthy way to foster the sustained onward growth of a church plant is to move as rapidly as possible to an equal partnership with the sponsoring church. Consequently, these strategies 4.3.ii-v, can be seen as stages on the road to this goal. They may be particularly useful when further financial resources are not available and therefore are directly responsive to the situation of the Church in recession.

4.5   It is also apparent that the more the parent churches share power and place trust in the plant, the more vigorous the growth in quality and quantity that results. Just as many churches have shown that generous and indeed sacrificial financial giving reflects the message of the New Testament, so a giving away of power is characteristic of responding to the call to evangelism in the act of planting churches.

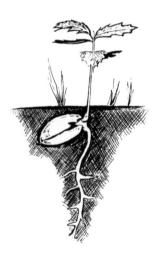

Part Five

TELLING SOME STORIES (1)
Plants within existing boundaries

5 Example (i): Three new congregations:
Runners of the pioneer type

5.1   A parish of about 22,000 people near the centre of a Northern city is characterised by industrial and domestic building including no fewer than seven distinct types of housing across the width of the social scale. In 1980, a team ministry was formed, effecting a merger between a strong church of 'low' church tradition and a weaker neighbouring church of a 'higher' tradition. The congregation in one of the churches has become the parent to three young church plants which are in varying stages of growth.

5.2   The decision to produce church plants stemmed from the report of a lay-led DCC working paper. Since both church buildings stand at the eastern border of the combined parish, main roads, railway lines and patches of industrial building have left a number of discrete communities unchurched for all practical purposes. In addressing this, the paper proposed that future staff be asked to focus on mission in these areas of the parish.

5.3   Initial plant
5.3.i   In one of these areas the church building had been demolished to make way for industrial development but in the event the area remained a chess board of small industrial estates and separated housing areas which still thought of themselves as relating to the previous church. The diocese agreed to the appointment of a team vicar 'with special responsibility for the inner city area' but without a church building. The diocese bought a house in a small housing estate which was being developed and the team vicar and four local church members from the parent church began to meet as a house group. A year later, the group invited their neighbours to meet with them for a monthly midweek act of worship. This led on to the first public Sunday service, held in the local primary school.

15

5.3.ii Unlike most recent church plants, evening as well as morning Sunday worship takes place. The services are held in the primary school. The morning service consists of informal all-age worship and teaching, without the use of books. The Bishop has given permission for the parish to use material from *Patterns for Worship* on an experimental, but renewable basis. At least half of the present congregation are new to the church. On three evenings of the month, the liturgy is 'Rite A' Communion with the words and songs projected onto a screen. The setting and style is more formal than in the morning and tends to attract a higher percentage of people used to traditional patterns of Church of England worship.

5.3.iii Although only four years old, this church plant has already begun to feel some of the pressures which fall upon those which begin with few and fragile resources. For example, all but one of the original team of four church planters have moved on. There have been difficulties in personal relationships, a shortage of lay leadership, and some unhappiness in the recognition and use of gifts for ministry. However, a small prayer and planning group has emerged. In not setting up a formal district church council, it has been possible to forward grassroots involvement in planning and decision making and this has proved crucial in bringing an unempowered culture forward.

5.3.iv It seems that five critical tasks remain to be addressed:

(a) to discover effective locally resourced ways of carrying out parish evangelism, since mission events with external partners have not been effective;

(b) to keep people who start coming to the morning worship, but who fail to be incorporated into the fuller life of the local church;

(c) to deal wisely and firmly with relationship problems in the congregation;

(d) to develop emerging shared leadership;

(e) to resist the temptation to provide a church building when the school is large enough and accepted in the local culture.

5.4. Second Plant

5.4.i When the Methodists withdrew, another particular area of the parish was left without a church. The diocese bought a house in the area and appointed a full-time curate who involved himself in community based activities. Two years later services began at festivals: Christmas, Mothering Sunday, Easter and Harvest. Festival services have drawn as many as fifty people. Later, monthly family services started on a trial basis in the local equivalent of a working men's club. In this pioneer work, the curate was assisted by a Reader from the parent church as a colleague. Of the ten regular Church of England worshippers who live in the area, five have wanted to commit themselves to the new venture, while five prefer to continue commuting to the parent church.

5.4.ii In this particular case, the church plant, which was quickly 'owned' by the local people, compensated to some degree for the sense of loss in the community caused by a history of urban decay, piecemeal planning, and by the church's previous inability to sustain a witness there. However, since the plant grew out of social involvement in the area, the church leaders are sometimes viewed as chaplains to the local community. There is, therefore, a danger that the church will be expected to give a religious veneer to what are effectively other people's agendas. If the first church plant might be thought of as a young child passing through a critical stage of growth, the second plant is more like a premature birth with attendant slow growth and a threatened existence.

5.4.iii Here, identified future tasks include the following needs:

(a) to form a weekly fellowship group to establish a base for future operations;

(b) to determine the appropriate future leadership of the church plant by consultation with both diocese and parish.

5.5 Third Plant

5.5.i In 1989, work began on a major housing development in a discrete area intended for 3,500 people. Akin to other urban housing developments it attracted similar buyers. Culturally and economically it is an anomaly within the parish and geographically distinct within it. The diocese agreed to purchase a house and then appointed a parish deacon, known informally as a 'Church and Community worker'.

5.5.ii As the development, conceived as a dormitory area, did not include any community facilities, the deacon worked from her home to care for the people of the neighbourhood. She intended to build a sense of community and to start a church when the time was right. Public worship in her house began early in 1993. She had built a motivated, and local, core team in order to hold together the evangelistic and social involvement dimensions of the Christian mission from the outset. In this case, the church plant has made its particular contribution to the area from the first and is like a healthy baby which still has a long way to go.

5.6 Comments

5.6.i Diocesan support, co-operation and facilitation have been important to the church planting programme in this example. The provision of staff and housing contributed materially to the well-being of the Church of England presence, as the city entered a period of urban regeneration.

5.6.ii The provision of a Team Ministry geared to church planting was also clearly helpful to both diocese and parish. It meant that clergy could be appointed and supported, without having attachment to existing church buildings, and were therefore free to pioneer new projects.

5.6.iii The Bishop was prepared to allow worship derived from *Patterns for Worship* on an experimental basis. This was helpful to the planters because the variety of cultural contexts in which church plants took place made them think more in terms of principle than strict adherence to liturgical forms. Indeed, rather than observe literal conformity to the texts, those marks of Church of England worship which are outlined in the report (p.5) have been acknowledged as a test of what is acceptable for the largely unchurched peoples who are reached through church plants.

5.7 Example (ii): A parish church reaches out:
A runner of the progression type

5.7.i Just north of a large industrial conurbation, a small mining community and surrounding rural area of 2-3,000 inhabitants has grown in a period of 120 years to a population of 12,000. The growth in number of the present congregation is inhibited because the building feels full when more than 100 people attend, which is frequently the case.

5.7.ii The church lies on the eastern edge of the parish. A western area of the parish contains an estate built in the late 1960s and early 1970s, together with some private housing around it. When the clergy raised the possibility of church planting as a call to the parish from God, it was welcomed by the more visionary women and played down by the more practical, cautious men in the congregation. The PCC, however, unanimously decided to take steps toward planting.

5.7.iii From the church membership of 120, 14 adults, including a Reader, and their children formed a core team. Nine members of the core group lived in the area, three in council housing. The group began to meet weekly with the new curate who happened to live on the estate in a house rented from the diocese. They began praying for the area and examining the teaching of the New Testament about the Kingdom of God and how this might work out in practice for their neighbourhood. They then became a 'pilot group', devising a strategy by which members of the parent church would visit every one of the 1,080 homes in the area prior to the official opening of the church plant in the local primary school. Ninety three people, nearly all from the private estate, attended the opening service. No-one transferred from other churches. Of those who started, 95 per cent continued to attend, and a few people from the council estate were added later.

5.7.iv From the outset, worship was identifiably of the Church of England, with both eucharistic and family services, and using material from the ASB printed on cards. The school was laid out as a church interior with altar, candles and frontals, and the clergy wore robes. As with other church plants, however, the services have an informal feel to them. Members have taken part in leading worship, although not officially licensed to do so. There is space for creativity in worship expressed through the use of meditation, drama and music.

5.7.v The mission work of the church, apart from the style of worship, continues through enquirers' groups, further visiting, and a longing to demonstrate the Kingdom of God in relation to the social needs of the neighbourhood. This includes addressing the problem of unemployment which has been running at 14 per cent.

5.8 Comments

5.8.i There are many issues surrounding this church plant. These relate to financial costs; the provision of ongoing ordained leadership; and the maturing process required to take the plant forward towards autonomy while it is still in a relation of interdependence with the parent church.

5.8.ii The costs of establishing the plant have not been small. It has cost £3,000 per year to hire the school. Administrative costs of launching the project have run into four figures. Nor is the school venue without disadvantages, since there is the weekly task of setting up the service, the caretaker jangles keys at 12.15 pm, and there is a lack of a convenient place to hold midweek activities. Fourteen of the more able members of the parent congregation have been given away to the plant, and the parent church has therefore felt bereaved of some key friends and workers.

5.8.iii A healthy church plant also raises problems for the diocese. As with other plants, the question soon arises as to how far they are to be clergy dependent and whether the diocese will be in a position to replace the existing staff upon which the plant has initially relied. Church plants often owe much to clergy in their first appointments, but these clergy tend to move on after three or four years. Although church plants commonly use unauthorized lay people to lead worship, this raises questions at diocesan level. This tendency also suggests that faster ways of recognizing, training and equipping gifts for ministry, either through a central ministerial foundation course set up by the diocese, or through local courses moderated and validated by the diocese, can be helpful. For example, a seven week course for lay worship leaders at church plants is being run by this diocese.

5.8.iv The particular problem for the parish lies in the development of the relationship between church and plant, between 'parent' and 'child'. The new, growing congregation of 55 adults and 42 children, poses most of the key questions, for example:

(a) How will parent and new church grow up into mutual interdependence and responsibility while avoiding a stultifying relationship of daughter to mother church? How can this interdependence be modelled so that the two congregations enrich each other?

(b) What effects will this have on the processes of government and administration employed, i.e. on the PCC and the 'pilot group'?

(c) How can finances be organized when the plant becomes self-supporting?

(d) What will happen about weddings and funerals if the plant flourishes, and how far should a planted congregation be led to expect that they will eventually have their own building and self-determining control?

(e) What expectations may members of a congregation have if they have only ever worshipped in a secular building such as a school hall, - should a local church plant have the ultimate aim of becoming the church for its area by becoming a parish in its own right?

5.9 Example (iii): a town-wide church planting programme

5.9.i In 1991, in a large town in the north west, a group of Church of England clergy were introduced to the idea of a strategy to 'disciple' the town. They received details of the strategy set out in DAWN (see Appendix 4) and a steering committee was set up to investigate the strategy further. Forty seven church leaders from across the denominational spectrum, including Roman Catholics, and representing forty churches, committed themselves to a town wide research project in preparation for a large Christian congress to be held in 1992. The 'surrounding community' and the 'church itself' provided the two fields of enquiry in the seven areas into which the town was divided. The research for this was done by the church members themselves.

5.9.ii The strategy depended on an undergirding basis of prayer, while the attempt to mobilize churches from being maintenance-oriented to thinking about mission focused on a public display of the research. When the results were presented in the town square, 5000 people visited the display, while during the Congress, 120 leaders gathered to agree preliminary goals for the churches during the remaining years of the decade. These included: producing 30 new worshipping communities; forming 700 home groups in the town; and getting 20 per cent of the population to attend church;

5.9.iii The Congress also agreed a 'Town Vision Statement' such that the town 'would become a Christ-centred town where every person can hear the good news of Jesus Christ in a way they can understand and that they can also see this good news lived out in churches, congregations and communities in every neighbourhood of the town'.

5.9.iv Following the Congress, Church leaders have been meeting in their respective areas to co-ordinate their evangelism. An annual census of the churches is being conducted to assist leaders in measuring the effectiveness of their strategy. Training in evangelism has been provided. A Forum for Christians in youth work was convened to confront the challenge to the churches of young people in the town.

5.9.v The method of this town-wide initiative has been designed to create an environment for church growth that will allow the churches to multiply after their own kind in a climate of mutual trust, respect and sensitivity. Communication between the churches has been enhanced and co-operation is being encouraged.

5.10 Comments

5.10.i Although in this town church planting was not often thought of as an option in the past, it is now seen by a growing number of churches as the best means of reaching the unchurched in a town area. Previously, anyone wishing to plant a church in the town might well have encountered suspicion, concern and even outright hostility from other churches and other denominations. This has been changing as churches recognize their common mission. The results of research have played a major role in creating a climate conducive to church planting.

5.10.ii The town strategy recognized that not all churches could or would want to consider church planting. By including them in the process, however, they have become as much part of the overall objective as the churches which will be expecting to plant congregations. The strategy has been as much about renewal and revival as it is about multiplication. By bringing together churches from across the broad spectrum of denominations, church planting has been placed openly on the agenda of the churches. This reduces the level of threat perceived by those who do not wish to participate in this particular form of evangelism.

Part Six

TELLING SOME STORIES (2)
Cross boundary plants

6.1 Anglican missiologists such as Henry Venn (d.1873) and Roland Allen (d.1947) encouraged the development of new Church of England congregations which would become self-supporting, self-governing and self-propagating as soon as possible. Recently, some Anglican church worshippers have planted congregations across parochial boundaries, but without the approval of either the bishop or the local incumbent. Neither Venn nor Allen would have approved of such a strategy because they believed that self-realization was not to take place at the expense of episcopal authority. To be members of the Church of England, clear local identity and responsibility must be matched with clear central accountability.

6.2 The examples in Part Five demonstrate that while church planting raises questions of various kinds which need to be addressed both by the dioceses concerned and by the individual parishes, the essential mission initiative is seen to be positive and encouraging.

6.3 In this section, examples of those church plants which have crossed boundaries are given. This is first to point up the similarities with the previous cases, such that the essentially vital and healthy desire to reach the unchurched is demonstrated, but this is also to address those particular concerns and sense of threat that have arisen as a result of the crossing. By placing these concerns in the context of what is necessary and good about church planting, it is possible to form a balanced and considered approach to attendant problems.

6.4 Example (iv): Multiple Congregations
6.4.i This case is included here as a pivotal and developing example, since three of its four congregations do not represent cross boundary plants. It is therefore essentially a contained initiative, out of which an unusual development has occurred.

6.4.ii Not far from the university buildings in the suburbs of an industrial city a well attended parish church has developed its premises to meet the needs of a growing and diverse congregation. The parish has become an LEP but, for the purpose of this report, it is interesting to note the use of the church building by multiple congregations. For example, on a Sunday morning, two congregations, each with a clear identity, meet at different times with different concerns, such as providing in one congregation for families with young children, and in the other, families with older children. Two other congregations, each with a different focus, meet on Sunday evenings. One is directed towards the young professionals and students. The other is an unusual church plant which is described below in more detail.

6.4.iii Consequently, four congregations meet in the same building each Sunday, each with their own leadership, style, music and teaching programme. Each congregation has its own set of house groups and pastoral care structures. For the sake of economy in scale and management, church administration and some church functions are shared. In this way, the clergy find themselves in a matrix system of leadership whereby they are generalists in their pastoral responsibilities for one of the four congregations, but also specialists in terms of their role in the wider church family. For instance, one of them holds overall responsibility for the policy making, resourcing and training of the house groups throughout the church. It is a Team Ministry and the Team Vicars lead each congregation.

6.4.iv The unusual fourth congregation constitutes a church plant which has begun to gain a life independent of the parent church. For example, a financial trust has been set up which rents the building from the PCC. Both the diocese and the parish have approved the moves which this congregation has been making towards becoming a parish in its own right. They have formed an acting PCC and elected acting church wardens. The congregation is therefore analogous to a young adult with a first job who is paying rent to the parental home while looking for independent lodgings. The plant is looking beyond the existing parish, from a situation where there can be no residents. It is located within another church's parochial boundaries, and aimed at the unchurched in the mainstream of modern culture who live anywhere within reach. Currently, this church plant is in contact with 28 other congregations which in one way or another are following the model, and of which about 60 per cent are of the Church of England.[8]

6.5   Comments

6.5.i The development of this situation has led to some interesting practical and legal questions. In order to address these, the congregation and the diocese have been looking for a suitable venue to house a large congregation, strategically placed in the city where it can best reach out to the network within the urban community it seeks to serve. This partnership springs from the determination of the congregation to retain a recognizably Church of England identity. The leadership of the plant is committed to this. For example, new believers in the congregation are confirmed by the bishop.

6.5.ii The proposal to have a church without a traditional parish, or a parish without a traditional church, represents an example of what might be called 'city centre ecclesiology'. The idea is not to establish another highly mobile student congregation, as a kind of additional informal chaplaincy, but a permanent, locally rooted eclectic church, as an officially approved departure from the traditional norm in the Church of England.

6.5.iii Resisting the view that they serve a sub-culture, the leaders of this particular plant argue with some force that whereas most Church of England churches actually serve a church-going 'sub-culture' within England, the plant's worship, which combines the atmosphere of traditional worship and the disco, reaches the cultural mainstream of the young in modern Britain, in a way most churches cannot approach.

6.5.iv In this case, then, the diocese is gladly assisting in the creation of a church plant which exemplifies the emphasis on network.

6.6   Example (v): re-planting a congregation:
A plant of the graft type

6.6.i Two suburban parishes, A and B, were conjoined to make one parish with an estimated combined population of 25,000, and with two

---

[8] During the completion of this report, a venue beyond the parish has been approved and the plant has moved out.

church buildings. The area is characterised by high mobility with a growing incoming population. Some years earlier the Deanery Pastoral Committee had suggested some kind of amalgamation and, when the vicar of parish B retired, the incumbent of parish A agreed to take responsibility, so long as the redundant vicarage and its site could be sold, and the proceeds directed to the re-ordering of the 19th century church building in which very few worshipped regularly at that time.

6.6.ii However, the desired re-ordering did not take place and eventually the vicar of parish A and a team of 25 members moved over to the poorly attended church in parish B, leaving parish A to continue to build up its own witness. They knew that failure to do so would leave some 12,000 residents without a Church of England presence. The grafted team comprised those who, it was hoped, would become severally a music team, a team of children's workers, a team of welcomers and a team to serve refreshments. The purpose here was to include those who had not yet been incorporated into the ministries of the sending congregation.

6.6.iii Although some money was spent on the building, it did not remove the signs of damp and decay, or improve the ancient heating system. However, a multi-racial congregation of about 100 people, a simple music group, an effective public address system, a coffee area, a bookstall, banners, a vested nave altar and a reading desk on a simple dais, all proclaimed that something healthy was taking root. A handful of people from the remainder of the local congregation returned to be part of the revitalized congregation.

6.6.iv There are therefore now two viable Church of England congregations offering a credible witness in a large parish. Congregation A is eclectic and congregation B is more local. In congregation A about 70 per cent of the church members come from beyond the parish boundaries. This is a particularly noticeable feature of demographic change, such that the parish now includes a vast resident Asian population, most of whom are unchurched. A successful evangelistic coffee shop set up to reach residents but situated in the eclectic shopping area, is indicative of the way congregation A has continued to build up an alternative community of Christians in a particular locality. Their focus has been on a church building not a bounded parish area.

6.6.v Parish boundaries are also largely meaningless to the local secular population. There is no longer a community that may be so-called in any meaningful sense. There are now many micro-communities based on common ethnic background or centred in a housing estate. In such a context, the church becomes a genuine alternative model which tries to transcend ethnic and social boundaries through a common commitment to Christ. In this suburb, members of the Church of England are trying to express this through one largely eclectic congregation, part of which is now grafted into another more local congregation.

6.6.vi The aim in making the graft was to provide in parish B a locally based, Christian worshipping presence and witness, largely multi-racial and ecumenical, with the support and help of an imported team from parish A. There are also other neighbourhoods within the two parishes in which it would be possible and indeed would be helpful to plant new congregations.

6.7 Comments

6.7.i In this suburb both congregations have that difficulty which all Anglicans face in conurbated areas, where traditional parish boundaries become irrelevant or meaningless, and grassroots ecumenism flourishes. Many urban dwellers do not think about crossing boundaries, of whatever sort, when they attend church. Mobility, however, brings with it both advantages and disadvantages. For example, the mobile team which accompanied the vicar as a graft into the receiving parish proved to be a group of mixed potential, many of whom were young people in their twenties. Some members of this group moved on, and others were replaced.

6.7.ii In this case, the diocese left the Church of England members to resolve their own problems. As has been seen, these centred upon the uncertain future of a deteriorating church building, and the failure to resolve the sale of the vicarage. There was also indecision about the use of the proceeds even if the sale were to be successfully concluded. Such uncertainty, and the absence of a purpose common to the thinking of both diocese and parish, can therefore be seen as a source of misunderstanding and unhappiness.

6.7.iii Another issue which compounds the uncertainty is the denominational make-up of the congregation in parish B. Many members are

'Church of England-friendly' but with little intention that they will become more than that. Without the legality imparted by being an official LEP, some fear that the congregation will leave as quickly as it arrived. Were it to become the first Anglican and Mar Thoma LEP, as is remotely possible, then doubtless this would be welcomed.

6.7.iv The problem of what appears to be an effective strategy of mission is further exacerbated by the question, often lurking behind many church planting initiatives, of who will succeed the initial leader. Staffing cutbacks could not only restrict the development of the graft but also inhibit further church planting in at least three other areas of potential within the parishes.

6.7.v The problems for parish and diocese may therefore be summarized as follows: use or disposal of existing buildings which are inappropriate for mission today; the future of grassroots ecumenical congregations; and the provision of ongoing leadership for local congregations whose vision includes church planting.

6.8 Example (vi): partnership as a strategy for church re-planting: A plant of the seed type

6.8.i A UPA near the centre of a Northern industrial city consists largely of tower blocks and has the second highest index of multiple deprivation in the city. The district church within the parish, in which 20 or 30 people continue to worship, is due for demolition. In this case, with the co-operation of the diocese, a partnership has been forged with a flourishing city church of a different churchmanship, in order to provide a way forward in the area.

6.8.ii The larger congregation is asked to contribute lay people, prayer, expertise, ideas and finances. The neighbouring parish has agreed to the area being designated a conventional district, and also to the appointment of a minister in charge by the larger congregation, but with the agreement of the local church representatives. For its part, the diocese will create the conventional district, pay the minister-in-charge as a team member of the larger congregation, and will provide suitable housing in the vicinity.

6.8.iii   The goal of the church plant has been outlined in the partnership document as: 'so to participate in evangelism and social action in the community in ways that are appropriate to the local culture as to help the church to discover an appropriate model for its own life and growth with a view to establishing St. L. as an independent parish'. It is hoped that the process will be completed in five to ten years.

6.8.iv   The relationship of St L. with the larger congregation is expected to move from one of foster child to a partnership and, eventually, to independence. Initially, a small number, around six, from the larger congregation will become members of St L. Others will offer ministerial skills on a temporary basis without becoming members. The permanent incomers will number fewer than the residual congregation, and this process is now under way.

6.9 Comments

6.9.i   At present there are few examples of this kind of cross-cultural urban re-planting, but sensitive partnership of this imaginative sort could offer the promise of much church regeneration. It demands what Alvin Toffler calls 'a new ad hocracy'. If it starts with dependence, it moves forward to partnership and ends in an independent congregation, but one which has learned to value interdependence and, one hopes, the importance of further reproduction in the course of time.

6.9.ii   A key to the outworking of the strategy is the principle of extended team ministry by which the vitality and gifts of a large congregation are harnessed for the benefit of one from which the life seems to be ebbing. In this case it operates within an essentially Church of England vision of a country-wide ministry for all, and through the connection of one parish with another, and with partner churches. However, it breaks with some tacit Anglican assumptions about parochial boundaries as comprising territory. It involves the identification of non-viable churches, the suspension of such livings and their incorporation into the ministry of a nearby growing church for a period of perhaps five to ten years.

---

[9]   The strategy, incidentally, is congruent with the line of Professor Robin Gill's thinking which he shared with the House of Bishops in June 1991. This is reproduced in his recent book, *The Myth of the Empty Church* (SPCK, 1993) in which he argues that subsidized parishes must be recognized for what they are and put on a mission footing which then can be evaluated and assessed.

6.10 Example (vii): an unauthorized church plant

6.10.i About 125,000 people live in a provincial town where, in Church of England parishes, 45 per cent of those on electoral rolls cross parish boundaries to go to church. In the 1980s a church which was itself a post-war church plant became full, planted a church, became full again, and wanted to plant another one.

6.10.ii An NSM member of staff began to look for a venue for an overflow congregation. Because many worshippers crossed parish boundaries in order to attend church, the congregation had established neighbourhood house groups in the discernible areas where clusters of church members lived. An enquiry was therefore made about the possibility of grafting a group of 60 members into another parish's congregation of 15 church attenders. This strategy proved abortive. The bishop was then approached about the possibility of using another church building in a different parish. Enquiries received a positive reaction from diocesan leaders. The arrangement proposed was for the NSM of the transplanted congregation to be licensed to serve under the local vicar whilst retaining his existing licence. It seemed a good way to link sending and receiving churches, and of preserving the authority of both incumbents. From the point of the sending church, the congregation saw it 'both as a way of relieving congestion and as a means of enabling some members to worship and witness more effectively in their own area'. The proposal met, however, with some hesitations within the receiving parish and, frustrated by the lack of progress, the church planters began to explore other possibilities as an interim move to finding somewhere of their own.

6.10.iii It was felt that, quite apart from practical difficulties, to use one of two possible Free Church venues in the area where church members lived would send ambiguous signals about the plant's identity. A local primary school, an attractive location to the two house groups meeting in the area, was much more promising and welcoming, but it was situated in a parish of a churchmanship different from that of the sending congregation, and the incumbent, having considered the proposal, could not welcome it.

6.10.iv Because the members of the proposed church plant still held out hopes that the diocese would approve their use of another town centre church building for which they had been negotiating, they only booked the local school for a two month period and weekly services began. The local vicar objected to the unilateral start and so the offer that the plant become a daughter church was not countenanced. As a consequence, the leaders of the embryonic church plant bound themselves to make every effort to move to another location. The bishop extended his permission when the search proved fruitless, and pending a discussion in the House of Bishops. However, the bishop moved elsewhere and felt reluctantly that the matter would have to be drawn to a conclusion before he left the diocese and recognition was withdrawn from the plant.

6.10.v The view of the diocese, and now of the sending parish, is that the ongoing congregation, still meeting in the local school, is an independent church with whom warm ecumenical relationships are to be maintained. The congregation, which has trebled since its illegitimate birth, feels frustrated by inflexible Church of England structures, defensive local clergy, and even the sending congregation which seemed to want them to go but, in the end, did not stand by them completely. In consequence, the worshippers, still using recognizably Church of England forms of worship, feel that they are in an ecclesiastical limbo.

6.11 Comments

6.11.i This cross-boundary plant began in the same way as others of the same sort where a group of worshipping Church of England members clustered in a defined geographical area tried to focus their life, service and witness through providing public worship on Sundays in that defined area. The purpose was not to break the traditional boundaries of other parishes but rather to build upon the Church of England's ecclesiological instinct to accept responsibility for an area and to foster the spiritual life and witness of church worshippers living there.

6.11.ii Conflicts arose because the inherited parish system sits uncomfortably with modern urban patterns of commuting across boundaries to attend church. Today, many people attend church through personal as well as through parochial links and set high value on choice and mobility. As a consequence, in urban Britain some choose to worship locally but others prefer to travel for family, friendship, cultural or churchmanship reasons. Church plants across boundaries are therefore bound to cause unhappiness with upholders of traditional understandings of the Church of England's parochial system. Here it is possible to see that the problem really lies not with 'church' but with 'plant', the transition from territory to network disturbs those whose thinking is necessarily grounded in territorial associations.

6.11.iii Some have wondered whether a return to the founding of proprietary chapels might prove a way forward. However, these were part of a process which looked to preserve particular Church of England traditions within historic parishes of a different viewpoint. Therefore a strategy has been chosen which sees church planting not as an isolated and particular phenomenon, but as part of mission strategy and Kingdom thinking as a whole.

6.11.iv One possible way forward would be for a diocese to create specially designated, 'underchurched' areas (see Part Three) and to re-direct redundant churches into the care of the deanery. Indeed a deanery mission strategy might well include the sharing of congregational resources in such a case. This would make more room for manoeuvre, and for the positive exercise of episcopal authority in partnership with local incumbents in the shared cure of souls. Where there has been approval on the part of all concerned, the problems of church planting across parochial, deanery and even diocesan boundaries have been overcome.

6.11.v In trying to establish whether a cross-boundary plant is still expressive of the Church of England, the following criteria may be helpful:

(a) is there commitment to the doctrine and practice of the Church England as expressed in the Declaration of Assent?

(b) do the members of the planted church come from within the neighbourhood or network which the plant is designed to serve?

(c) is there evidence of a desire to reach out to the unchurched in the defined neighbourhood or network?

(d) do the leaders of the planted congregation display an affirming attitude to other traditions around them?

(e) do they use authorized forms of worship, being those allowed by bishop's authority under section B of the Canons of the Church of England?

(f) do the leaders of the congregation have episcopal ordination, licence or authorization to exercise their ministries in the local church and do those ministries include a life and teaching consonant with those normally experienced within the Church of England?

(g) does the congregation acknowledge episcopal leadership, and accept financial and other diocesan obligations and generally participate in the common life of the diocese?

6.11.vi It should be stressed that these criteria should not be used as part of an ecclesiological fundamentalism which disowns any venture that departs slightly from the norm. On that basis, a number of long established parishes would be in severe difficulties. On the other hand, notable departure in any one of these seven areas must be taken as a significant indicator that a plant is hardly serious in its claim to be part of the Church of England.

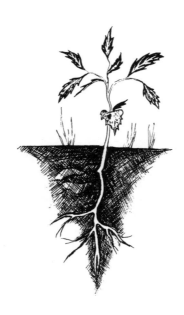

Part Seven

WHAT IS ALLOWED?

7.1   Because church planting, as has been seen, is an organic and reproductive process which involves people, it is inevitable that there will be tension with structures not designed to cope with mission strategies which involve neighbourhood and network.

7.2   The strategies and case studies above indicate that questions are likely to arise in a number of important categories, especially: the authorization of ministers, forms of worship, administration of the sacraments, buildings, boundaries and ecumenism. This section attempts to address some of the legal issues involved.

7.3   Matters relating to 'church'

7.3.i   Authorization of ministers

(a)   It is essential that adequate provision is made for the leadership of a church planting team, whether ordained, lay or both. Such leadership needs to be identifiable and authorized.

(b)   Where a church plant takes place across parish boundaries the rights and responsibilities of the incumbent of the receiving parish need to be recognized. The incumbent shares with the bishop the responsibility for the 'cure of souls' in the area. The incumbent's permission is needed before incoming clergy can exercise ministry within the parish concerned (see Canon C 8 para. 4). There are exceptions in the case of certain ministry within the homes of persons on the electoral roll of parishes belonging to incoming clergy and in the case of colleges, schools, hospitals and public or charitable institutions (see Canon B. 41.2). It would not be feasible, however, to extend these extra-parochial exceptions to church plants. The *Extra-Parochial Ministry Measure,* (1967), section 1, specifically excludes in the former case 'the performance of any office or service attended by persons other than the members of the family and household of the person whose name is on the electoral roll'.

(c)   A pattern of Group or Team Ministry can be a help here. Clergy are quite often appointed to a team without attachment to existing buildings. Where there is already a collaborative ministry in an area it is relatively easy to add the minister leading the church plant to the group. A group arrangement may be more flexible than a team; it allows incumbents the possibility of working within one another's parishes, and would provide the legal framework for church planting in the future. On the other hand it is possible to add one or more Team Vicar posts to a Team. Sections 20-22 of the *Pastoral Measure* (1983) deal with Teams and Groups.

7.3.ii. Liturgical questions

(a) A number of issues are highlighted by the church planting movement. Ideally, a new church plant will attract those who do not normally attend worship. If, for example, the planting congregation comes from a parish church situated in a middle-class area and accustomed to traditional forms of worship, but the new plant is in a local authority housing estate where most of the population do not habitually read there will need to be careful planning to ensure that the worship in the new congregation is reasonably accessible. Questions relating to worship and its accessibility are not of course limited to church plants or to local authority housing estates; accessibility is a proper goal for every congregation, but what it means in practice will vary according to context. This report has given examples of the use of experimental material, such as from *Patterns for Worship*, with episcopal permissions.

(b) In the case of licensed buildings the bishops have power to direct which forms of service shall be held, and which are not required (see Canon B 11A). Canon B.40 lays down the requirement of the Bishop's permission for the celebration of Holy Communion other than in a consecrated building within the minister's cure or other building licensed for the purpose.

(c) The approval of *A Service of the Word* and *Affirmations of Faith* by General Synod in November 1993 will bring even greater flexibility, while the proposed revisions to Canon B11 include the provision for the minister of a parish to invite a 'suitable lay person' to lead certain forms of worship.

7.3.iii. Administration of the sacraments

Where the church planting team does not include the appropriate licensed ministers, special provision will have to be made. The administration of Holy Communion by extension may be appropriate (see Canon B 12 para. 3).

7.4. Matters relating to 'plant'

7.4.i. Buildings

(a) New congregations need to find places where they can meet for worship, unless they plan to meet in an existing church building. It may not be possible or desirable, for financial or other reasons, to erect a new church, at least in the initial stages. Some church plants have used rooms in schools, public houses or other secular buildings. The diocesan bishop has authority to license such buildings, or a part of such buildings, for public worship. Further, under the 1983 *Pastoral Measure* (section 29 (2)) the Bishop 'may designate any church in any parish ... or any building or part of a building licensed for public worship as a parish centre of worship'.

(b) It is not essential for a parish to have a parish church (see section 17 (4) of the 1983 *Pastoral Measure*). In such a case however there may be a parish centre of worship. Possibly there could be several centres of worship in each parish, including the schools and other secular buildings mentioned above. Centres of worship can be used for baptisms, funerals, weddings and Holy Communion. They do not have to be consecrated or conform to any particular standard of construction although for obvious reasons, size, access and safety aspects would dictate the suitability of individual locations.

(c) This potentially affects church planting in two ways; the plant can have its building recognized as a parish centre, whether or not a new parish is created, and if one is created it does not need to have a parish church erected.

7.4.ii. Boundaries

(a) There are occasions when some alteration to parish boundaries will be beneficial. An example would be the case of a church plant in a new housing area which overlaps more than one parish. Where all interested parties are prepared to give consent the changes can be made without much delay.

(b) It is also possible to form a conventional district out of one or more parishes, although such a district has limited legal status and the agreement has to be renewed with every change of incumbent. These limitations could, however, be beneficial at the early stages of a church plant, and this approach has been most often used where the plant provides for a substantial area of new housing.

(c)   While the 1983 *Pastoral Measure* is not specifically tailored for the issues arising out of church planting, many of its provisions are relevant. It gives a remarkable number of possibilities for change, including —

the alteration of parish, deanery or diocesan boundaries

* the union of two or more benefices

* the union of two or more parishes

the holding of two or more benefices by one incumbent

* the formation of a new benefice and/or parish

* the formation of team or group ministries

* *These require the longer procedure leading to a Pastoral Scheme.*

(d)   Section 17 (1) (d) of the 1983 *Pastoral Measure* provides for the creation of new 'extra-parochial places'. Such places have traditionally been, for example, army camps (*Army Chaplains Act,* 1868) or places like Launde Abbey. Although this provision may not have been intended to facilitate church planting, it may have a role to play. However, there will be other important matters (for example in relation to the application of the Church Representation Rules) which will require careful consideration.

(e)   Some have also argued for an extension of the principle of proprietary chapels, but many would see these as anachronisms often set up as a focal point of differentiation from the parish church. The tidiest solution is to create a new parish, though this raises questions of patronage and definition of the extent of the boundaries of the new parish.

7.5   Ecumenical Considerations

7.5.i.   When a church plant is an ecumenical project, for example in a new housing area, the bishop of a diocese has a specific role as described in *Ecumenical Relations – Canons B43 and B44: Code of Practice.* In the case of the formal establishment of a Local Ecumenical Project, there are definite procedures to be followed (set out in paragraphs 54-57 of the *Code of Practice* on pages 13-16). However, there are many ways in which local ecumenical co-operation may gradually evolve and a subsequent rule of good practice suggested by Churches Together in England is that: 'when member churches are reviewing existing work or considering new work they should share their proposals for action with other member churches through the relevant ecumenical body'.[10] This may be seen to apply equally to plans to plant a church as to any other activity or project.

7.5.ii.   Canon B43 covers all situations, which are not formal ecumenical projects, in relation to those churches to which this Canon applies, designated by the Archbishops of Canterbury and York. The Church of England *Ecumenical Relations Measure* and Canons B43 and B44 have made possible the 'sharing of ministry', without implying full interchangeability of ministries, while the *Sharing of Church Buildings Act* (1969) has facilitated the sharing of buildings and has enabled the growth of ecumenical co-operation.

---

[10]   *Working Together in the new Ecumenical Instruments*, Principle 2.

Part Eight

GUIDANCE

8.1 It has been shown that church planting is a mission strategy which involves living and vital processes which in each case are necessarily unique to the situation. For this reason, it is impossible to contain all the important possibilities which church plants offer within a set of guidelines. This section therefore offers guidance on the assumption that sensitive consultation will always provide the best results where church planting is an option.

8.2 Church planting normally involves the establishment of a new congregation or worship-centre and is to be encouraged as an important part of Church growth. It can, however affect the ministry of other churches and denominations and the staffing of the area even when it takes place within the parish of the planting church. Early consultation is therefore essential.

8.3 The material in this section applies to the inception of church plants, but it is important to realize that church planting is not a one-off activity. Once a church is planted, the congregation must grow and evolve. Therefore this report also contains further guidance for those later stages in a plant's evolution, which may appropriately be included as part of a review structure. This further guidance can be found in Appendix One.

8.4 Strategic planning

8.4.i Church planting should normally be the result of long-term diocesan planning in partnership with the deanery concerned and with other Christian churches. It should not only be the result of the vision and initiative of the planting church(es). Bishops may have an important role in initiating, sustaining and encouraging the planning process.

8.4.ii Such planning should normally include a Mission Audit process which will discern which areas and networks have little or no contact with the existing church and which congregations have the resources to plant. (See the criteria for underchurched areas in Part Three).

8.4.iii Where a congregation desires to plant because it has grown too big for the building or is of a size that impedes a proper sense of community or further growth, and where there is not an area suitable for church planting within the same parish, alternative possibilities should be considered. It may be possible for a second autonomous congregation to worship in the same building but at a different time. If a significant proportion of the congregation resides in other parishes some might work with their local parish church with the consent of both their own incumbent and that of their local church, in order to build up the life of the Church there. It may be appropriate to initiate discussions on the possibility of planting or transplanting in a different parish.

8.5 Consultation

At the earliest possible stage there will need to be full consultation where applicable, with:

(a) the Archdeacon and Rural or Area Dean and through them the appropriate Pastoral Committee(s). The implications for future staffing needs should be taken into account;

(b) the Diocesan Adviser on Mission and Evangelism;

(c) the leaders of other denominations through the Diocesan Ecumenical Officer and the appropriate body of the County Churches together;

(d) other local congregations;

(e) civic, local and community leaders and groups.

8.6 Buildings

8.6.i It may be useful to explore all the possibilities for using existing buildings at an early stage. When a new congregation is fully established and its financial situation clear, it may be appropriate at this stage to look at the possibilities for new church buildings.

8.6.ii Advice should be sought from the bishop on whether the building to be used for worship should be designated a 'centre of worship'.

8.7 The church planting team and its accountability

8.7.i Joint oversight and accountability should be agreed, whether or not the leader is in priest's orders. Local oversight is the ultimate responsibility of the person who shares the 'cure of souls' within the boundaries of the parish concerned with the bishop, even if this is temporarily delegated by agreement. Similarly, the PCC remains ultimately responsible for all legal and financial matters. Care needs to be exercised in the recognition of leadership. This is not just a local church concern but the diocese must be consulted.

8.7.ii The church planting team should be carefully selected, trained, authorized and supported. It should normally have a mixed membership, according to class, gender, age and ethnicity as appropriate.

8.8 Preparation and Education

Training to develop cultural awareness, enhance sensitivity and to promote accountability might be arranged where appropriate, with the help of diocesan resources.

8.9 Worship

8.9.i The bishop's approval should be obtained where there is to be a celebration of Holy Communion in a building which is not consecrated or licensed for public worship (Canon B.40).

8.9.ii In areas where the majority of the population have no church background there may be the need for flexibility in patterns of worship, at least in the initial period. In such cases the bishop should be consulted as to whether it is appropriate for him to exercise his powers to permit such flexibility (Canon B 11A). The aim should, however, be to work towards a recognizably Church of England form of worship. In ecumenical projects, worship should be consonant with recognized denominational styles.[11]

8.10 Ecumenical Involvement

8.10.i This should be encouraged from the start wherever possible.[12]

---

[11] See *Ecumenical Relations, Canons B34 and B44: Code of Practice* (1989), Section C: Commentary and Guidelines on Liturgical Matters.

[12] The Council for Christian Unity has produced a booklet, *Opportunities for Unity*. It contains fifteen suggestions for parishes and a pull-out section of '101 things to do together'.

The Council for Christian Unity has also produced *Ways of Working Together: Information and Questions for Local Ecumenical leadership* (February 1994).

The Group for Local Unity (GLU) of Churches Together in England produced a booklet, *Guidelines for the Review of Local Ecumenical Projects* (1991). There is also a document: *Constitutional Guidelines for a Local Ecumenical Project* (Revised [interim] December 1993).

Alongside *Working Together in the New Ecumenical Instruments: Suggested Rules of Good Practice* (CTE), and *Ecumenical Relations, Canons B43 and B44: Code of Practice* (1989), there is ample material to hand which illustrates the new way of working together.

8.10.ii Where an ecumenical plant is desired, the county ecumenical sponsoring body[13] will help local churches in drawing up a Declaration of Intent, but this will eventually need to be accompanied by a working Constitution. For Local Covenants and other LEPs, as for single church plants, there are marks of maturity to look for, which will include matters of:

(a) mission
(b) ministry and worship
(c) growth and development
(d) generation of new members
(e) financial viability and giving
(f) relationships with the wider Church

The plant or LEP should not, however, be expected to comply with more stringent standards than those expected of other local churches.

8.11 Pastoral Reorganization

Formal Pastoral Reorganization may be necessary at some stage, especially where the plant takes place across parochial or denominational boundaries. It may be appropriate to make the plant a conventional district, to alter parish boundaries, or to set up a team or group. The first of these alternatives can be a useful temporary stage.

8.12 Constitutions

Because each plant is unique and does not conform to a blueprint, this guidance does not include a specimen Constitution. It may be helpful to draw up agreements between planting and planted churches in some situations and between the diocese and the planting parish. Any such agreements which are drawn up should refer to all or some of the categories mentioned above, perhaps in particular to buildings, leadership, administration, financial obligations to the diocese, decision-making, appraisal and review, relationship to planting church, relationship to other partners or congregations, liturgy and worship.

---

[13] For information about local ecumenical sponsoring bodies, contact either the revelant Diocesan Ecumenical Officer, or The Council for Christian Unity, Church House, Westminster, SW1P 3NZ.

Appendix One

WHAT HAPPENS NEXT?

A1.1 Interviews with those who have planted churches, together with second hand knowledge of further instances, lead to the observation that the quality and continuity of the plant's leadership is the single most influential factor in determining the success of a planting venture. The provision of such a leader and the assured continuity of leadership, over at least five years ahead, are the greatest gifts a diocese can make to a new church plant.

A1.2 This and other dimensions of growth, learned by hard experience, can be turned into recommendations for dioceses and planters alike. What follows are not hard and fast rules, but an expression of reasonable expectations for healthy church plant development. To assist a new initiative such as a church plant, it is better to have some longer term aims, even if they are not all fulfilled, than to have none at all. At the least, some questions about bringing a plant to maturity are pertinent, and planters and diocesan officers can sit down together and think through the future using this material as a basis for their work.

A1.3 We emphasize that these recommendations are not be to be applied inflexibly, for all parties need to bear in mind the diverse patterns of planting and vastly differing resources available to different plants. For example, each territory, neighbourhood or network will have its own degree of openness, or resistance, to the ministry of a new church plant. Moreover, those groups with slender resources need to pass through an initial stage of growth towards maturity, which is not always necessary for others which begin from greater numerical strength and gifts in ministry.

A1.4 It can be helpful therefore, to think of three key stages of development in the life of church plants, bearing in mind the different resources available in each individual case:

(a) beginning from a small group

(b) the first five years of a small congregation

(c) the second five years after planting a small congregation, or starting with a congregation of more than 50 members.

A1.5   Beginning from a small group:

This could apply to pioneer plants of all types

This stage is characterized by growth through outreach from a small mission team – normally fewer than seven people – to a larger group, and then to a small congregation of about twenty members. Until the small congregation coheres, a plant may be vulnerable and may lack stability through having to absorb new members and through having to adjust to their needs.

A1.5.i   LEADERSHIP

In this case the authorized leader of the plant needs to possess pioneering evangelistic gifts and the ability to train others to share this ministry. A prime task in this stage is for the entire team to build contacts and friendships with those outside the group. In doing so, it is important that the discovery and enabling of gifts in ministry should be encouraged, so that the congregation can begin to function effectively. Also, before the launch of public worship it is helpful if there can be identified leaders for: children's work; a worship team; house groups and nurture groups.

A1.5.ii.   WORSHIP

Throughout the life of any plant, its worship may be in tension between culturally attuned worship and authorized Church of England practice. This applies to all three stages (A1.5, A1.6, A1.7) in this appendix.

A1.5.iii   BUILDINGS

While the plant is still in the stage of being a group, it will probably meet in a house or in a rented room of a secular building. This will have to be reviewed at the point where it becomes a small congregation. A bridge between group and congregation stages can be effected by forming two groups, but this depends on an assured quality of leadership and on common purpose.

A1.5.iv   GOVERNMENT, ADMINISTRATION AND FINANCE

(a) Formal structures, such as district councils, may not be the best way of proceeding at this stage. The plant is still embryonic, the membership may not be settled and in some underchurched areas what may be seen as an hierarchial model can be alienating. The plant may benefit most if financial obligations to parish and diocese should be kept at a minimum throughout this stage and it is expected that the plant will be supported by the budget of the receiving parish.

(b) It may take one to five years to achieve all the steps necessary to become a small congregation and this should be taken into account when deciding on the timing for review.

A1.6 The first five years of a new/small congregation: This could apply to progression plants of all types

This stage is characterized by progress from an official launch of a small dependent congregation (20-50 people) to the formation of church with a clear self-recognition and identity and some autonomy, expressed as District, Team or Conventional District status. The expectation of numerical growth should be to between 60-100 adults, with attendant growth in Christian maturity.

A1.6.i LEADERSHIP

(1) It is advisable that the authorized leader have evangelistic gifts and the ability to train others in this ministry, at least for the first five years or until the number of regular adult attenders exceeds fifty. By the end of this period, if the leader is a curate in priest's orders, that person can be designated a Team Vicar to ensure greater continuity of leadership. Where the plant is lay led, exploration of LNSM can be helpful.

(b) Training people to lead is inevitably important for growth and ecumenical or Anglican forms of tutored distance learning can be explored where the combination of evangelism and training will place heavy burdens on the leader. Similarly, the congregation should be encouraged to advance beyond fifty members, since this is often noticeably a sticking point for some small congregations. This can be done by continued evangelisation and by keeping church organizations to a minimum. New members joining after the plant's inception should be helped to share the founding vision and missionary identity of the congregation.

(c) Before the launch of public worship, it is essential to have designated leaders of the following: children's work; worship team; house groups and nurture groups.

(d) Towards the end of five years or when numbers of attending adults regularly exceeds fifty, thought may be given to a different mix of gifts in the authorized leader. Where it is not obviously appropriate to have fresh leadership the leader's gifts may be supplemented by a lay team.

A1.6.ii BUILDINGS

(a) It is preferable that the building used for worship be rented, not owned, as numerical growth is a high priority and may force a change of venue. Also the costs of ownership and maintenance may be damaging to a small congregation's purse and confidence. However, in new towns or large private housing developments the cultural expectation and provision of diocesan finance may make a desired church building possible.

A1.6.iii GOVERNMENT, ADMINISTRATION AND FINANCE

(a) By the end of five years the plant should aim to be financially self-sufficient for all running expenses, including up to the equivalent of half the cost of a stipend.

(b) The most helpful way of paying the diocesan quota is through some form of agreed relief. For example, the assessment could be made on attendance figures collected for two years previously, as a high proportion of attenders will be fringe people whose purses are by no means dedicated to the plant.

(c) Within five years, a district church council will probably have been formed and there will be sizeable representation on the parent PCC. An alternative will be to create a conventional district. Whatever form of government and self-determination will be in tension between Church of England and local cultural norms.

(d) This stage may take 2-5 years to complete.

A1.7 Five to ten years after planting a small congregation:

This could apply to the second five years of progression plants starting with congregations of over fifty and to all transplants

The characteristic of this phase is growth towards an interdependent, mature adult church within the diocesan patterns of parishes, being self-governing, self-financing and having the potential to reproduce where appropriate. With all but some rural plants, growth should be expected to reach 120-200 adults and well as growth in depth and maturity. Such maturity may be signalled by the ability to produce leaders, disciples and to offer gifts to the wider church, as well as the potential to reproduce once more.

A1.7.i LEADERSHIP

(a) The authorized leader for this stage should ideally have gifts in pastoral care, public teaching and administration. If the original plant leader has these gifts, s/he may most usefully continue to oversee the plant's continued growth. If not, that person's gifts may be better used in a further new plant and a fresh leader, standing the same tradition, can be appointed.

(b) By the beginning of this stage, a lay-led plant, should look to have some form of ordained leadership. A team of leaders, at least one ordained, should be built up to provide the basis for further sustained growth and to facilitate any further planting.

(c) Evangelisation remains the continuing task of the congregation.

(d) The future allocation of ordained staff should take equal note of congregation size as of parish size, – that is, it should take serious account of the shift from territory to neighbourhood and network.

A1.7.ii BUILDINGS

(a) During this period, demands for a building that is owned and which feels more ecclesiastical may be made. How suitable this change is for continued evangelisation of the neighbourhood, culture or network, will have to be carefully considered, as will the financial considerations.

(b) Large transplants usually inherit a church that is redundant, involved in pastoral re-organization or facing imminent closure. Sensitivity is required in forming a relationship with any residual congregation and without compromising the mission initiative of the incoming group.

A1.7.iii GOVERNMENT, ADMINISTRATION AND FINANCE

(a) Throughout this period it is particularly helpful if the diocese can encourage the parent congregation to release the plant from dependent status, and the plant can form an acting PCC. All permanent financial subsidy from the parent church should cease when this point is reached, and the diocesan quota will be payable on the normal rate with an agreed relief in respect of new fringe members. By the end of the period the planted church should be able to become a parish.

(b) At this point, there should be consultation with the diocese to consider and to assist any plans for a further plant from this new church.

Appendix Two

IDENTIFICATION OF PLANTS

	RUNNERS		GRAFTS		TRANS-PLANTS		SEEDS	
	Progression	Pioneer	Progression	Pioneer	Authorised	Unauthorised	Progression	Pioneer
Is the plant within the existing parish?	Yes	Yes	No	No	No	No	No	No
Is the plant team greater than 20 members?	Yes	No	Yes	No	Yes	likely	No	No
Is there a residual congregation in the planted area?	No	No	Yes	Yes	Yes	Yes	Yes	No
Has there been permission to plant across a boundary?			Yes	Yes	Yes	No	Yes	Yes
Is the residual congregation more numerous than the planters?			Yes	Yes	No		Yes	
Is the planting team the major partner in the planting work?			No	No	Yes		No	
Does a significant number of the planting team live in the church plant area?	Yes	No	Yes	No	Yes	Yes	No	No
Do plant members relocate?	No	maybe	No	maybe	No	No	Yes	Yes

Appendix Three

STATISTICS

A3.1 The statistics quoted in the text and in this section have been gathered since 1985 by the Revd George Lings at the request of the Day Conference for Church of England Planters, held biennially at Holy Trinity Brompton in London. Information is supplied to him in response to advertisement, through the Church Press and through personal contacts of those within the evolving informal network of those interested in church planting. While virtually all the information has been received first hand, there is no claim that it is exhaustive.

The figures are correct at November 1993.

A3.2 Number
Since statistics began to be collected in 1985, 177 church plants are known to have begun, 116 of these occurring within the last five years. Since 1990, the average rate of church planting has been 30 per year, at least one per fortnight.

A3.3 Location
Nearly all dioceses contain at least one church plant, though it is noticeable that only 5 plants have occurred in rural areas; all the others are in towns or cities. 60 per cent of all church plants are in areas with a 'strong' church presence, such as in areas of private housing. 40 per cent have occurred in 'weak' church areas. 16 per cent of church plants have taken place in the suburbs; 12 per cent in Urban Priority Areas; 15 per cent on local authority housing estates and 7 per cent in inner urban areas.

A3.4 Relation to parish boundaries
79 per cent of the church plants remained within the parish boundary. Thirty five of the plants (21 per cent) crossed a parish boundary and of these 31 took place with full consent. There have therefore been 4 unauthorized plants. 92 per cent of plants remained within the deanery and 98 per cent within the diocese of the sending parish.

A3.5 Buildings

(a) 107 plants (65 per cent) have rented schools, community centres or other public buildings, while 50 (30 per cent) have used existing churches and church halls. Eight plants (5 per cent) occur in houses, usually because of the lack of public premises.

(b) Because church planting is an organic process, it is significant that the attempt to collect statistics about the actual plant's characteristics show particular variation. For example: planting teams may be small (2) or substantial (100+); partnership with neighbouring parishes may involve the plant occupying a senior, equal or junior role; the maturity of the plant at any stage may be various depending on the degree of autonomy reached; the needs of the receiving area may condition whether the plant may be classed a 'pioneer' or 'progression' type. It is precisely that the needs of the 'church' in a church plant may be variable that may cause boundaries to be crossed and different venues to be found.

(c) It is important to note that the unique combination of all these factors in the status of a church plant conditions what may be termed the 'planting dynamic' or mission emphasis of a plant, and that this unique character of a plant must be understood by the diocese.

Appendix Four

DAWN: Discipling A Whole Nation

A4.1   DAWN is a movement which seeks to unite denominational and parachurch leaders in a process of prayer, research, planning, leadership training and church planting. Its underlying vision is to work towards a church for every neighbourhood and cultural group within the nation. The strategy was first developed in the Philippines and Guatemala. In 1988, DAWN launched a programme in New Zealand involving several denominations, including Anglicans, and where, its proponents believe, it has halted the decline among the denominations. The strategy begins with the formation of a national committee followed by research and analysis to determine those areas in the country concerned that are underchurched. A congress is held for both denominational and parachurch leaders and each denomination sets its own goals and develops plans to achieve them, working ecumenically and co-operatively wherever appropriate or possible.

A4.2   A DAWN conference of leaders was held in Birmingham in February 1992, to which denominational representatives were invited. The conference divided into denominational streams and as a result the Methodist Conference last summer set the target of an average of one new congregation per circuit by the year 2000. The Baptist Union similarly has set targets. Unfortunately the conference clashed with General Synod and therefore there was only part-time unofficial representation from Church of England synodical structures, though Anglicans represented the largest number present. Whatever form of official involvement is practicable, it is certainly desirable; it needs to be determined whether specific goals can be set for the Church of England.

The programme in this country has so far used the title 'Challenge 2000'.

A4.3 The DAWN programme in the Philippines has also produced ten principles of polity, which may be useful in looking at a church planting situation. These principles include consideration of:

(a) responsible pluralism

(b) mutual respect

(c) evaluation of proximity of new and existing groups in relation to density of population

(d) unity and diversity

(e) team spirit and fellowship

(f) sharing resources

(g) reaching the unreached

(h) reconciliation

(i) local church, organization and parachurch relationships

(j) common planning

A4.4 The story at section 5.10 of this report illustrates the outworking of DAWN principles in a town in this country. Challenge 2000 reports that some 50 other cities, towns and districts have begun local DAWN-type consultations.